COURTSIDE DEVOTION

Copyright © 2024
by UFaith Hoops

All rights reserved. No part of this publication may be reproduced, distributed, or transmitted in any form or by any means, including photocopying, recording, or other electronic or mechanical methods, without the prior written permission of the publisher, except in the case of brief quotations embodied in critical reviews and certain other noncommercial uses permitted by copyright law.

ISBN 9798320074511

Book Cover by UFaith Hoops

www.ufaithhoops.com

DEDICATION

To every athlete navigating the highs and lows of competition: remember that your identity is rooted not in victories, statistics, or applause, but in the unchanging love and purpose of Christ.

To those who face pressure, setbacks, and quiet moments of doubt: may your heart remain anchored in God, your focus unwavering, and your decisions guided by integrity and faith. To the leaders on and off the court: rise with courage, serve with humility, and inspire others through a commitment to excellence that reflects something far greater than the game itself.

To every reader of *Courtside Devotion*: may these pages equip you to compete with purpose, stand firm in your faith, and navigate every challenge with clarity, strength, and confidence.

UFaith Hoops

CONTENTS

Introduction-7

Chapter 1: Overcoming Your Shooting Slump-9

Chapter 2: Wait With Patience-15

Chapter 3: Finding Strength In Adversity-19

Chapter 4: Finding Peace In Pressure-25

Chapter 5: Overcoming Anxiety Through Faith-29

Chapter 6: Strength In Weakness-33

Chapter 7: Boldness In Sharing Your Faith-37

Chapter 8: Finding Rest With Athletic Demands-41

Chapter 9: Letting Go Of Overthinking-47

Chapter 10: Trusting God's Unique Plan-51

Chapter 11: The Waiting Season-55

Chapter 12: Finding Strength And Focus In God-61

Chapter 13: Finding Balance-65

Chapter 14: Comfort In God's Presence-71

Chapter 15: Finding Hope In God Through Struggles-75

Chapter 16: Prioritize Your Time With God-79

Chapter 17: Finding Confidence In God-85

Chapter 18: Seeking Unity And Peace Within Team-91

Chapter 19: Overcoming Bad Habits Off The Court-97

Chapter 20: Finding Strength In Defeat-103

Chapter 21: Soaring On Wings Of Faith-109

Chapter 22: Finding Strength In Recovery-115

Conclusion-121

INTRODUCTION

Competition tests more than just speed, strength, and skill; it also challenges character, focus, and the decisions made when no one is watching. *Courtside Devotion: For Christian Athletes* is designed to guide you through these moments, helping you anchor your heart in God as you navigate the pressures, challenges, and victories of sports. Just as your body requires training to perform at its best, your mind and heart need intentional preparation to compete with purpose and integrity.

Inside these pages, you will find prayers, reflections, and Scripture passages designed to challenge, inspire, and equip you to remain steadfast on your journey. Each day offers an opportunity to grow in faith, build resilience, and make decisions that honor God amid competition. Whether you are a professional athlete, a student athlete, or simply passionate about sports, these devotionals will help you navigate pressure, setbacks, and success with clarity, strength, and confidence.

Courtside Devotion is a playbook for life. It teaches you to rise above distractions, handle adversity with grace, and lead with integrity. By committing to this journey, you prepare to excel not only in sports but in every arena of life, standing firm in your faith, confident in your purpose, and equipped to leave a lasting impact.

OVERCOMING YOUR SHOOTING SLUMP

Discover Renewed Confidence On The Court With God

Have you ever found yourself in a shooting slump where no matter how hard you try, you just can't seem to work yourself out of it? Use these 6 practical steps below to navigate this time with God:

Step 1: Remember Your Identity In Christ

Scripture: *"I can do all things through Christ who strengthens me." - Philippians 4:13*

As an athlete, experiencing a shooting slump can challenge both your confidence and perseverance, often creating the feeling that you are not reaching your full potential. However, it is important to remember that your worth and identity are not defined by your performance on the court but by who you are in Christ. Take a moment to reflect on this truth and find comfort in knowing that God is with you, providing you with the strength needed to overcome any challenge.

Step 2: Trust God's Timing

Scripture: *"But those who wait on the Lord Shall renew their strength; They shall mount up with wings like eagles, They shall run and not be weary, They shall walk and not faint." - Isaiah 40:31*

In times of struggle, athletes may be tempted to seek quick solutions, such as taking endless extra shots in frustration, overanalyzing every release, or pushing harder without addressing the underlying issue. Yet, God's timing is always perfect, and He promises to renew our strength when we wait on Him. Place your trust in His plan, believing that He will guide you through the shooting slump with grace, patience, and wisdom.

Step 3: Practice Perseverance And Patience

Scripture: *"Let us not become weary in doing good, for at the proper time we will reap a harvest if we do not give up."*
- Galatians 6:9

As you navigate this shooting slump, stay committed to your training, remain disciplined in your efforts, and trust that the work you invest will bear fruit in due time. Persevere through the challenges and setbacks with confidence that God is shaping you through this season of struggle. Keep your focus on Him and wait patiently as He continues to work on you.

Step 4: Seek Support And Encouragement

It is essential to surround yourself with a strong support system during times of struggle. Reach out to teammates, coaches, and loved ones for encouragement and guidance. Allow them to pray for you, offer advice, and uplift you during this difficult season. Remember, you are not walking this journey alone; there are people who genuinely care about your well-being, both on and off the court.

Step 5: Focus On The Process, Not The Outcome

While it is natural to desire immediate improvement and success, it is crucial to shift your focus from the end result to the process of growth and development. Celebrate small victories along the way, whether it be an extra hour of practice, a slight improvement in your shooting form, or a positive mindset shift. Have confidence that God is at work in every detail of your journey, and recognize that each step forward, no matter how small, contributes meaningfully to your overall growth and progress.

Step 6: Embrace A Growth Mindset

Instead of viewing this shooting slump as a setback, see it as an opportunity for growth and learning; a season that can strengthen your resilience, character, and faith. Approach each practice and game with a positive attitude, a willingness to learn from mistakes, and a steadfast commitment to improvement, allowing these challenges to shape and refine you. Trust that God is at work during this difficult season, using it to develop you into the athlete and person He has called you to be.

Remember that God is with you every step of the way. He has a purpose and plan for your journey both on and off the court. Remain steadfast in your faith, trust in His timing, and continue to press forward with determination and grace.

Prayer For Champions

Heavenly Father,

I come to you in the midst of this shooting slump, feeling discouraged and unsure of how to overcome it. Help me to remember my identity in Christ, to trust in Your perfect timing, and to practice perseverance and patience as I work through this challenge. Please provide me with the strength and wisdom I need to push through this season and bring glory to Your name through my actions on the court. Thank you for always being with me and guiding me through every trial. In Jesus' name, Amen.

REFLECTION

WAIT WITH PATIENCE

For The Athlete Suffering From
Lack Of Playing Time

It can be disheartening when you are not getting the playing time that you desire. It is natural to feel discouraged and question whether your hard work and dedication are being recognized. However, true encouragement comes from understanding that your value is not measured by playing time or external recognition, but by your identity and purpose in Christ.

In 1 Corinthians 12:12-14, the apostle Paul reminds us that just as the body is made up of many parts, each with its own unique function, so too are we as members of the body of Christ. Limited time on the court does not diminish the importance of your role on the team. Time on the sidelines can be just as meaningful as time in the game, offering opportunities to support and encourage teammates, develop patience and perseverance, and trust in God's timing and plan for your life. Rather than dwelling on what seems lacking, focus your energy on becoming the best teammate, the most encouraging supporter, and a consistent example of Christ's love in all that you do.

In addition to supporting your teammates and trusting in God's plan, it is important to remember that struggles and challenges are opportunities for growth and character development. Use this time to refine your skills, maintain your physical conditioning, and strengthen your focus and mental approach to the game. Take advantage of the opportunity to seek guidance from coaches and mentors, request constructive feedback, and set meaningful goals for your ongoing development.

Additionally, use the extra time off the court to engage in activities that bring you joy and fulfillment. Invest in relationships with loved ones, pursue hobbies, personal interests, and prioritize both your physical and mental well-being. Remember that your identity and value extend beyond athletic performance and are rooted in who you are as a Believer.

By focusing on your overall growth, you will not only enhance your abilities as an athlete but also strengthen your character and resilience. Trust that God has a plan for you and that every experience, whether on the sidelines or in the game, is shaping you into the person He intends you to become. Remain faithful, maintain a positive outlook, and continue to give your best in all you do, knowing that God sees your heart, effort, and has a meaningful purpose for you both on and off the court.

Prayer For Champions

Heavenly Father,

I come before You seeking strength as I face limited playing time. Remind me that Your plan is greater than my frustrations and that You have a purpose for me both on and off the court. Strengthen my heart to uplift my teammates with joy, even when it is difficult. Teach me patience and help me trust Your timing with faith. In Jesus' name, Amen.

REFLECTION

FINDING STRENGTH IN ADVERSITY

A Devotional For The Athlete Suffering From An ACL Injury

Scripture: *"And we know that in all things God works for the good of those who love him, who have been called according to his purpose." - Romans 8:28*

Suffering a season-ending injury, especially one as severe as an ACL tear, can be challenging both physically and emotionally. During these times, it is natural to question God's plan and wrestle with doubt. However, Scripture reminds us in Romans 8:28 that God works all things together for the good of those who love Him, even amid hardship and disappointment.

Although the purpose of this trial may not be immediately clear, it presents an opportunity for growth, resilience, and character development. God can use this period to refine your perseverance, strengthen your faith, and shape you into the athlete and individual He has called you to be, demonstrating that His plan encompasses far more than the circumstances we face in the moment.

Despite the physical limitations that come with your injury, remember that your worth and value as a person are not defined by your athletic abilities. God sees you as His beloved child, and He is with you every step of the way. Use this time of rest and recovery to draw closer to Him, seeking His guidance and strength in the midst of your struggles.

As you continue on this journey of recovery, remember that God has a purpose for everything that happens in your life. Your injury may be a setback right now, but it can also be an opportunity for growth and renewal. Instead of dwelling on the negative aspects of your situation, try to focus on the positive lessons that you can learn from this experience.

During periods of rest and recovery, the most important step is to remain anchored in God through prayer, asking Him for guidance, strength, and clarity in the midst of your challenges. Ground yourself in Scripture that speaks to endurance and perseverance, allowing His truth to shape your perspective as you step back from competition. Use this time to strengthen your faith, reassess your priorities, and prepare for what lies ahead with renewed focus. Trust that even in stillness, God is at work. His presence provides direction, stability, and purpose that extend beyond recovery into every area of life.

While navigating the ups and downs of healing, remember that your identity is not defined by your athletic ability, performance, or current limitations. Your true worth is rooted in Christ alone; you are His child, fully loved and accepted regardless of your achievements. Recovery is not wasted time; it is a season in which God refines your character, strengthens your faith, and realigns your perspective. Use this period to draw closer to Him through prayer, Scripture, and reflection, allowing His grace to renew your mind and His love to anchor your heart. In doing so, you will not only regain physical strength but also develop greater confidence in who you are in Him, a foundation that no setback can shake.

In prayer, seek patience and perseverance so that you may face this trial with steady faith and courage. Ask God to strengthen your resolve to honor Him not only when progress is visible but also when the process feels slow and difficult. Trust His perfect plan, remembering that every detail of your life is under His control and guided by His wisdom. Let your response to setbacks, whether in competition, training, or recovery, be a testimony of trust and obedience that brings glory to His name.

With every step on the road to recovery, take confidence in the presence of God, who guides, strengthens, and sustains you through each challenge. Place your trust fully in His sovereignty, relying on His wisdom and timing, even when progress feels slow or uncertain. Hold firmly to His promises, knowing that His faithfulness is constant and that He will never abandon or forsake you. Allow this assurance to shape your perspective, granting you patience, perseverance, and renewed purpose as you navigate every stage of healing.

Prayer For Champions

Heavenly Father,

I come before You in this season of uncertainty and struggle, lifting my injured body to You, asking for healing and restoration. In the midst of disappointment and frustration, help me find peace and strength in Your presence. Remind me that my identity is secure in You, not in my performance or abilities. Let this time of adversity become a season of growth and renewal that draws me closer to Your love and grace.

Grant me patience to wait on Your timing, perseverance to endure this trial with courage, and faith to trust in Your perfect plan. Give me the wisdom to recognize Your hand at work in every detail, and the humility to surrender my ambitions to Your will. May I glorify You not only in competition but also in how I respond to setbacks and challenges. Thank You for Your constant love and sustaining grace that carry me through every trial. In Jesus' name, Amen.

REFLECTION

FINDING PEACE IN PRESSURE

For The Athlete Struggling With The Pressure To Perform

Scripture: *"But seek first his kingdom and his righteousness, and all these things will be given to you as well."*
- Matthew 6:33

The pressure to perform can often feel overwhelming, as expectations, scrutiny, and the constant pursuit of success weigh heavily on your shoulders. In those moments, it is easy to believe that your value is tied to your performance. However, your identity is not measured by points scored, minutes played, or the approval of others. It is defined by your relationship with God, who has already called you His own.

God calls us to seek His kingdom first, above all else. When we place our faith and trust in Him as our highest priority, every other area of life, including our performance as athletes, finds its proper place. The abilities we possess are not accidental; they are gifts entrusted to us by God for the purpose of bringing Him glory. When we surrender our performance to Him, we are freed from the burdens of comparison, fear, and pressure. Instead of striving to prove ourselves, we can compete with confidence, knowing that the outcome rests in His hands and that our role is simply to give our best as an act of worship. Every moment on the court, whether marked by victory or defeat, is an opportunity to honor God and reflect His presence through the way you compete.

In moments of doubt or insecurity, turn to the promises of Scripture and let them steady your heart. God's love for you never wavers, and His purpose extends far beyond the scoreboard. Trust in His sovereignty, knowing that every circumstance is part of His design to shape you into the person He has called you to be.

When the pressure to perform feels overwhelming, turn to God in prayer. Ask Him to steady your heart, renew your strength, and grant you clarity in the moment. Trust His perfect plan for your life, knowing that He is present with you in every challenge and every step forward.

Remember, your identity is not determined by your performance, but by the unchanging love and grace of God. Keep seeking His kingdom first, and watch as He brings abundance and blessings into your life. God is with you always, guiding you, supporting you, and cheering you on in all that you do. Trust in Him, seek His righteousness, and know that He will never leave your side.

Prayer For Champions

Heavenly Father,

Thank You for the gifts, talents, and opportunities You have entrusted to us as athletes. Teach us to fully surrender our performance to You and to keep Your kingdom as our highest pursuit. Grant us the strength to compete with integrity, the peace to face pressure with confidence, and the wisdom to remember that our true worth and identity are found in You alone. In Jesus' name, Amen.

REFLECTION

OVERCOMING ANXIETY THROUGH FAITH

A Guide For The Athlete Struggling With Anxiety

Your journey as an athlete involves more than just training your body and sharpening your mind; it is also about discovering the strength and peace that come from God alone. When pressure increases and anxiety threatens to disrupt your focus, remember that you are never alone in the struggle. God is with you in every moment, offering His steady hand and guiding you through His Word so you can compete with confidence and clarity.

In Philippians 4:6-7, the apostle Paul delivers a powerful message: *"Don't worry about anything; instead, pray about everything. Tell God what you need, and thank him for all he has done. Then you will experience God's peace, which exceeds anything we can understand. His peace will guard your hearts and minds as you live in Christ Jesus."* This scripture reminds us to present our worries to God through prayer, confident that He will guard our hearts and minds with a peace beyond comprehension; one that no circumstance can take away.

When anxiety begins to rise, pause and turn to God in prayer. Present your concerns to Him, asking for His strength and the steady peace that only He can provide. Remember that He is in control, and His purposes for your life, including your journey as an athlete, are intentional, meaningful, and perfectly timed.

Hold firmly to the certainty of God's promises, and lean on the strength of His unfailing love and grace when anxiety seeks to overtake you. Allow His presence to quiet your spirit and bring calm, trusting confidently that He is faithfully guiding you through every step of your journey.

Prayer For Champions

Heavenly Father,

In moments of anxiety, fear, and uncertainty, we turn to You, seeking refuge in Your steadfast love and unchanging grace. Teach us to fully release our worries and entrust our lives into Your hands, confident that Your plans for us are perfect, purposeful, and far beyond our understanding. Grant us a peace that transcends circumstances, steadying our hearts and minds, and equip us with the strength, courage, and resilience needed to face every challenge. Thank You, Lord, for Your constant presence, guidance, and faithful provision. In Jesus' name, Amen.

REFLECTION

STRENGTH IN WEAKNESS

For The Athlete Struggling To Remember Their Playbook

In the intensity of the game, when the pressure is high and your mind struggles to recall the play, feelings of overwhelm and doubt can quickly take hold, challenging your confidence and testing your resilience. Even in the midst of these difficult moments, God's strength becomes most evident; sustaining, guiding, and empowering you to rise above the situation.

Drawing from 2 Corinthians 12:9-10, we're reminded of Paul's words: *"But he said to me, 'My grace is sufficient for you, for my power is made perfect in weakness.' Therefore, I will boast all the more gladly about my weaknesses, so that Christ's power may rest on me. That is why, for Christ's sake, I delight in weaknesses, in insults, in hardships, in persecutions, in difficulties. For when I am weak, then I am strong."*

Paul's insight speaks directly to the experiences of every athlete who has faced frustration and self-doubt. Just as Paul found strength by acknowledging his weaknesses and relying on Christ's power, we too can gain confidence and reassurance in the truth that God's grace fully sustains us, even in areas where we feel inadequate. Instead of allowing ourselves to be consumed by frustration and defeat, we can choose to surrender our struggles to God. By acknowledging our limitations and leaning on His strength, we open ourselves up to experience the transformative power of His grace.

When a coach's instructions feel overwhelming or expectations seem impossible to meet, it is important to remember that God's perspective far surpasses human judgment. While coaches evaluate performance and outcomes, God sees the heart and understands the full extent of your effort, dedication, and passion. He recognizes the discipline you bring to practice, the perseverance you demonstrate in competition, and the integrity with which you play; qualities that cannot always be measured by statistics or results. By maintaining this perspective, you can face every challenge with confidence, knowing that your true value lies in His approval, not in the praise or criticism of others.

Through prayer and reliance on God's strength, we can navigate through the challenges of the game with a renewed sense of purpose and determination. Let us offer our weaknesses to God as a testament to His power working within us, and may His grace empower us to rise above every setback.

Prayer For Champions

Heavenly Father,

In moments of weakness, frustration, and uncertainty on the court, we turn to You as our source of strength and wisdom. When our efforts fall short or our confidence wavers, remind us that our worth is not defined by performance but by Your unchanging love. Teach us to view setbacks not as failures but as opportunities to rely more fully on Your grace and to grow in perseverance. In Jesus' name, Amen.

REFLECTION

BOLDNESS IN SHARING YOUR FAITH

For The Athlete Afraid To Share God's Word Around Teammates

As you strive for both faith and athletic excellence, moments of uncertainty and hesitation may arise; especially when sharing your beliefs with teammates who do not share the same outlook. The possibility of rejection or misunderstanding can feel intimidating; however, Scripture reminds us that God has not given us a spirit of fear. Instead, He has equipped us with power, love, and self-discipline (2 Timothy 1:7). This truth empowers us to stand firm in our faith, speak with grace, and lead by example, even in challenging environments.

In Romans 1:16, Paul confidently proclaims, *"For I am not ashamed of the gospel, because it is the power of God that brings salvation to everyone who believes..."* His declaration reminds us that the message of Christ is not something to be concealed or compromised but embraced and shared with bold conviction. For athletes navigating a culture that may dismiss or challenge their faith, this verse serves as both encouragement and a calling. To stand unashamed of the gospel is to recognize that its power surpasses performance, reputation, and acceptance; it is the very hope that transforms lives.

Trusting the guidance of the Holy Spirit enables you to

engage in conversations about Christ with grace, humility, and confidence. The goal is not to argue or force persuasion, but to sincerely share your walk with God and the transformation you have experienced. A life marked by genuine love for Christ and others serves as a powerful testimony, drawing hearts closer to the truth.

In Matthew 5:16, Jesus instructs us, *"In the same way, let your light shine before others, that they may see your good deeds and glorify your Father in heaven."* Your actions both on and off the court can reflect the love and grace of Christ, creating opportunities for meaningful conversations and connections with teammates.

So, as you lace up your shoes and step onto the court, pray for boldness and sensitivity to the leading of the Holy Spirit. Be intentional about building authentic relationships with your teammates, showing them the love of Christ through your words and actions. Remember, you are not alone in this journey. God goes before you, equipping you with everything you need to share His love with those around you.

Prayer For Champions

Heavenly Father,

We ask for the courage to share our faith openly, even in moments when it feels uncomfortable or costly, trusting that Your Spirit will grant us the wisdom we need. Teach us to speak with both conviction and humility, so that our words are motivated not by pride but by love that reflects Christ. In our interactions with others, let our actions embody the weight of our faith, demonstrating integrity, patience, and compassion that point beyond ourselves to You. May every conversation and every example of our lives serve as a witness that draws others closer to You. In Jesus' name, Amen.

REFLECTION

FINDING REST WITH ATHLETIC DEMANDS

Reset With God In The Midst Of Athletic Demands

As the demands of a season intensify, it can become difficult to give proper attention to rest. The physical strain of training and competition combined with the mental pressure of performance often leaves little room for true recovery. However, Scripture reminds us that rest is not a luxury but a God-given necessity, essential for both renewal and endurance. By honoring this rhythm of rest, we align ourselves with His design for strength, balance, and wholeness.

In Matthew 11:28-30, Jesus declares, *"Come to me, all you who are weary and burdened, and I will give you rest. Take my yoke upon you and learn from me, for I am gentle and humble in heart, and you will find rest for your souls. For my yoke is easy and my burden is light."* This passage reveals that lasting rest is not just physical relief but a profound renewal found in Christ Himself. He offers peace for the mind, strength for the body, and restoration for the soul, reminding us that true rest is ultimately secured in His presence.

In athletics, it's crucial to recognize the significance of rest in optimizing your performance and overall well-being. Just as you train and push your body to its limits, you must also prioritize rest as an essential component of your athletic journey. Allow yourself time to recharge, relax, and rejuvenate, knowing that God desires for you to find rest in Him. Remember that rest is not a sign of weakness, but a necessary part of the process to become the best version of yourself, both on and off the court. Rely on God's wisdom and provision as you seek rest amid the demands of your schedule, confident that He will sustain and strengthen you throughout your athletic journey.

Athletes are often characterized by their relentless work ethic and pursuit of excellence, pushing themselves through demanding practices, grueling training sessions, and the pressures of competition. This commitment is essential for growth and success; however, without proper rest and recovery, both the body and mind eventually reach their limits. True peak performance is not achieved through constant exertion alone but by embracing balance; recognizing that rest is a necessary component for sustaining strength, focus, and endurance over time.

Just as we are called to pursue our athletic goals with focus and determination, we are equally called to honor our bodies by giving them the time and care they need to heal and recharge. Ignoring signs of fatigue or pushing beyond physical and mental limits can lead to injuries, prolonged recovery, and a decline in overall performance. Prioritizing rest is not a sign of weakness; it is a strategic choice that protects both physical health and long-term athletic potential. Beyond the body, intentional recovery nurtures mental clarity, emotional stability, and resilience, enabling athletes to approach each practice, game, and challenge with renewed energy, focus, and purpose. Recognizing and respecting these rhythms ensures that our efforts remain sustainable and aligned with the stewardship of the life and gifts God has entrusted to us.

As you progress through your athletic journey, pay close

attention to warning signs indicating that your body and mind may require rest. Notice persistent soreness, chronic fatigue, reduced motivation, or diminished focus. These are not signs of weakness but clear signals that recovery is necessary. Listening to these cues allows you to respond intentionally, preventing injury, preserving performance, and maintaining long-term health. Recognizing and respecting your body's limits demonstrates wisdom and discipline, enabling you to return to training and competition stronger, more focused, and fully prepared to perform at your best.

It's natural to fall into the trap of believing that rest is a luxury reserved for those who have already achieved success, but we must remember that rest is not a reward for the victorious, but a vital component of the journey toward greatness. Athletes who prioritize rest are better equipped to handle the physical, mental, and emotional demands of their sport, leading to improved performance and longevity in their careers.

As you strive for excellence in your athletic pursuits, remember that rest is not a sign of weakness but a mark of wisdom and stewardship over the body God has given you. Honoring your need for recovery is an investment in both your performance and overall well-being. Make rest a deliberate and essential part of your training, understanding that it strengthens you to compete with focus, endurance, and mental clarity. Trust that God sees your diligence, supports your rhythm of work and rest, and equips you to pursue your goals with sustained strength and purpose.

Prayer For Champions

Heavenly Father,

We come before You with hearts that are weary and in

need of rest. Help us prioritize caring for our bodies and minds amidst the demands of our athletic season. Grant us the wisdom to recognize our limits and to find true renewal and peace in Your presence. May Your unfailing love and grace be our strength, sustaining and restoring us as we entrust our athletic journey into Your hands. In Jesus' name, Amen.

REFLECTION

LETTING GO OF OVERTHINKING

Finding True Peace In Your Game Through Christ

Do you find yourself overthinking during the game or replaying moments afterward? The pressure to perform, fear of making mistakes, and constant analysis of every action can weigh heavily on your mind. Today, we encourage you to release these burdens and place your trust in God's plan for your athletic journey, knowing that He sees your effort and guides every step you take.

In Matthew 6:34, Jesus says, *"Therefore do not worry about tomorrow, for tomorrow will worry about itself. Each day has enough trouble of its own."* This verse encourages us to focus on the present, approaching each practice, repetition, and game one step at a time. Instead of becoming consumed with what might go wrong or trying to anticipate every possible outcome, we are called to surrender our worries to God and trust in His guidance throughout our athletic journey.

God has equipped you with the skills, talents, and abilities necessary to excel in your sport. He has placed a passion for the game within you and given you a platform to glorify Him through your performance. When the pressure of competition or the temptation to overthink every move arises, remember that He is with you in every moment; guiding your decisions, shaping your mindset, and directing your actions on the court. Trust in His provision and lean on His guidance, allowing yourself to perform with confidence, clarity, and purpose rather than being weighed down by fear or doubt.

When overthinking begins to overwhelm you, pause, take a deep breath, and turn your thoughts to prayer. Invite God into your mind and heart, asking Him to bring clarity, peace, and calm. Surrender the game, the outcomes, and every worry into His hands, trusting that He is in control and has a perfect plan for your journey. By doing so, you can release anxiety and perform with focus, confidence, and purpose.

Prayer For Champions

Heavenly Father,

We thank You for the gifts, opportunities, and passion You have entrusted to us. When our minds are clouded by worry or overthinking, help us to surrender our fears to You and trust fully in Your perfect plan for our athletic journey. Let clarity, peace, and calmness guide our thoughts, and remind us that every skill, every decision, and every moment is a blessing from You. May our hearts remain grateful, and may all that we do reflect Your presence and bring glory to Your name. In Jesus' name, Amen.

REFLECTION

TRUSTING GOD'S UNIQUE PLAN

Stop Comparing Your Journey; God Called You To Be Different

Comparison is a challenge that many athletes face, especially in a culture that frequently measures success by external achievements and standards. It is easy to fall into the trap of comparing your progress to that of teammates or competitors, which can lead to feelings of inadequacy, envy, or self-doubt. However, God's plan for your athletic journey is unique, intentionally designed to develop your character, gifts, and purpose according to His perfect wisdom.

"There are different kinds of gifts, but the same Spirit distributes them. There are different kinds of service, but the same Lord. There are different kinds of working, but in all of them and in everyone it is the same God at work." (1 Corinthians 12:4-6). This passage serves as a reminder that each athlete's abilities and strengths are uniquely given by God, and that no two paths are the same. Your talents, role, and journey in sports are intentionally designed to reflect His purpose, calling you to focus on the gifts He has entrusted to you instead of comparing yourself to others.

Rather than measuring yourself against others, focus on embracing the unique path God has entrusted to you, recognizing that comparison only distracts from His work in your life. Every athlete's journey is marked by different challenges, opportunities, and seasons of growth. God uses each one to shape character and purpose in distinct ways. Trust in His timing and provision, understanding that both success and struggle serve as tools He employs to refine you. Your worth is not tied to achievements or recognition but is firmly grounded in your identity as His child, created with intention and called to glorify Him through the gifts He has given you.

Prayer For Champions

Heavenly Father,

We come before You with honest hearts, acknowledging how often we fall into comparison and doubt. Remind us that You have written a unique story for each of us, and that the gifts You have placed within us are sufficient for the calling You have given. Teach us to celebrate others with joy while finding peace and confidence in the role You have entrusted to us. May our journey in this game always reflect trust in Your plan and gratitude for the purpose You have set before us. In Jesus' name, Amen.

REFLECTION

THE WAITING SEASON

For The Athlete Waiting On The Contract

Waiting for a new contract or playing opportunity can be one of the most challenging seasons in an athlete's career. The silence between phone calls and the uncertainty of what comes next can fuel frustration, self-doubt, and the temptation to take matters into your own hands. However, waiting is not inactivity; it is a space where God develops patience, strengthens perspective, and equips you with resilience for the challenges ahead. Instead of viewing this period as a setback, you can embrace it as preparation, trusting that the same God who gave you your gifts will also open the right door at the right time.

In seasons of waiting, Psalm 27:14 offers clear guidance: *"Wait for the Lord; be strong and take heart and wait for the Lord."* This call is not passive; it requires strength, courage, and steadfast trust in God's timing. Although the desire for immediate answers or breakthroughs can feel overwhelming, we are reminded that His plans unfold with precision and purpose. Instead of viewing waiting as wasted time, we are invited to use it as an opportunity to pursue God more deeply, seek His will with greater clarity, and allow our faith to be refined through patience and perseverance.

Remember that God not only sees the desires of your heart

but has also established a plan for your life that is greater than what you can perceive in the present moment. Jeremiah 29:11 affirms this: *"For I know the plans I have for you,' declares the Lord, 'plans to prosper you and not to harm you, plans to give you hope and a future."* This promise reminds us that even in seasons of waiting, God's hand is at work, preparing the way forward. As you continue to train, stay disciplined, and position yourself for future opportunities, anchoring your confidence in the truth that God is orchestrating every detail with perfect timing. Waiting is not wasted; it is where faith is refined, character is built, and breakthroughs are prepared according to His will.

In the stillness of waiting, there is an opportunity to discover meaning and intentional purpose. Rather than viewing this period as a delay, approach it as a season of preparation and refinement. Use this time to reflect on your journey thus far and realign your goals with God's plan for your life. Embrace the quiet as a chance to listen to God's voice and discern His direction. Remember, even in waiting, every moment serves a purpose.

Patience is more than simply enduring a period of waiting; it is the ability to wait with composure and trust. As you navigate this season of uncertainty, develop patience while placing full confidence in God's provision. Rely on the assurance that He knows what is best for you, even when the path ahead seems unclear. Use this time to increase your dependence on God and strengthen your faith, remembering that His timing is perfect and His promises are unfailing.

When facing uncertainty and the tension of waiting, remember that you are not alone on this journey. God has surrounded you with a community of fellow Believers who offer encouragement, prayer, and accountability during both challenging and ordinary moments. Lean on one another for support, drawing strength, insight, and perspective from the shared experience of faith. As Proverbs 27:17 teaches, *"As iron sharpens iron, so a friend sharpens a friend."* This reminds us that together we grow stronger, more resilient, and better equipped to navigate periods of waiting. Through mutual support, patience, and grace, you can endure seasons of uncertainty with confidence, trusting that God is working in and through every circumstance.

Seasons of waiting can test our focus and resilience, but they also provide an opportunity to strengthen our discipline and refine our abilities. Approach this time with intentionality; develop your skills, maintain your fitness, and sharpen your mindset so that when opportunities arise, you are ready to act with confidence and purpose. True success belongs to those who persist with diligence and patience, even in the face of uncertainty.

Lean on the support of those around you and remain attentive to God's guidance at every step. Trust that He is directing your path, orchestrating events with precision, and preparing you for what lies ahead. Be strong and take heart, knowing that His timing is perfect and that every effort, every moment, and every season work together to fulfill His good and perfect plan for your life.

Prayer For Champions

Heavenly Father,

We come before You with hearts patiently awaiting Your perfect timing for the opportunities ahead. Help us to trust in Your provision and plan for our lives, even when uncertainty and doubt weigh heavily upon us. Grant us strength, courage, and perseverance as we remain faithful during this season of waiting. May Your will be done in every step we take, and

Your glory be evident in all that we do. Guide our actions, refine our character, and prepare us to embrace the doors You open with confidence and gratitude. In Jesus' name, Amen.

REFLECTION

FINDING STRENGTH AND FOCUS IN GOD

For The Athlete Struggling To Concentrate

Amid the demands of training and the pressures of competition, maintaining focus can be a constant challenge. Distractions and moments of wavering attention may arise, pulling you away from your purpose. In those moments, the Word of God serves as your anchor, providing strength, clarity, and direction to keep you steady and grounded.

Scripture reminds us in Hebrews 12:2 to fix our eyes of Jesus, the author and finisher of our faith. To fix our eyes on Christ means to direct our attention and allegiance toward Him so that His character, His words, and His work on the cross shape our priorities and define success. Practically, this involves beginning and ending our efforts in prayer, recalling Scripture when distractions arise, examining our motives, rejecting comparison, and choosing obedience over outcomes. Our confidence does not rest on mental toughness alone but on His sustaining grace. When our focus rests on Him, clarity cuts through the noise, perseverance grows under pressure, and we remain aligned with the path God has marked out for us.

When your focus begins to waver or your mind drifts, take intentional time to pause and realign through prayer. Seek God's strength to provide the discipline, clarity, and concentration needed to perform with excellence and reflect His glory through your efforts. Rely on His presence and guidance to equip you with confidence and faith as you navigate challenges and overcome obstacles.

Remember that God has already equipped you with the strength and resilience to press forward and run the race set before you. As you remain rooted in His Word and seek His presence daily, you will discover the focus and endurance needed to overcome distractions and remain steadfast in your pursuit of excellence. In doing so, your journey becomes more than a personal achievement; it becomes a testimony of His power working through you.

Prayer For Champions

Heavenly Father,

In times of challenge and distraction, we turn to You for strength and guidance. Help us fix our eyes on Jesus, the author and finisher of our faith, and grant us the endurance to run the race You have set before us. Provide us with focus, clarity, and discipline so that our efforts honor You and reflect Your glory. In Jesus' name, Amen.

REFLECTION

FINDING BALANCE

Thriving In Academics And Athletics

The life of a student-athlete is characterized by competing priorities; academic responsibilities, athletic commitments, and personal development. Success in these areas requires more than effort and organization; it demands discipline, focus, and a mindset that aligns your actions with a greater purpose. True excellence is measured not only by grades or performance but also by the intention behind your work and the integrity with which you pursue it.

Colossians 3:23-24 offers guidance for this pursuit: *"Whatever you do, work at it with all your heart, as working for the Lord, not for human masters, since you know that you will receive an inheritance from the Lord as a reward. It is the Lord Christ you are serving."* As you balance your responsibilities as a student and athlete, remember that every assignment, practice, and game is an opportunity to honor God. When your efforts are rooted in Him, your work carries a purpose beyond immediate results.

Even as the demands of academics and athletics increase, God provides the wisdom and strength we need to navigate them effectively. James 1:5 says, *"If any of you lacks wisdom, you should ask God, who gives generously to all without finding fault, and it will be given to you."* This verse reminds us that when we face decisions about time management, priorities, or handling stress, we are not alone. By seeking God's guidance in prayer, we gain the clarity to make wise choices and the confidence to rely on support from teachers, coaches, and mentors as we balance our responsibilities.

Remember that your academic pursuits are just as important as your athletic endeavors. While basketball may bring moments of excitement, competition, and recognition, education provides the foundation that will support you long after the final buzzer sounds. Your commitment to learning equips you with knowledge, discipline, and critical skills that extend far beyond the court. Approach your studies with the same dedication and intentionality you bring to your training and competition, recognizing that a well-rounded education broadens your opportunities, shapes your character, and prepares you for the calling God has placed on your life both within and beyond athletics.

As you strive for excellence in both academics and athletics, it is essential to prioritize your well-being; physically, mentally, and spiritually. Adequate rest, proper nutrition, and intentional self-care form the foundation for sustained performance, both in the classroom and on the court. Equally important is nurturing your faith through consistent prayer, reflection on Scripture, and fellowship with other Believers. Trusting in God and relying on His guidance equips you with the endurance, focus, and perseverance needed to face challenges and respond to setbacks with confidence and purpose.

Furthermore, remember that your identity is not defined solely by athletic performance or academic achievements. Your true value and significance come from being a child of God, deeply loved and cherished. Regardless of setbacks or victories, low grades or honors, God's love for you remains steadfast and unchanging. Rest in the assurance that your worth is rooted in Him, and let this truth guide your confidence and perspective in every area of life.

In conclusion, as you navigate the challenges of balancing academics and athletics, anchor yourself in faith, discipline, and perseverance. Rely on God's guidance and provision, draw strength from the support of your community, and approach each challenge as an opportunity for growth and learning. With focused commitment and a steadfast spirit, you can excel both in the classroom and on the court, using your talents to honor God in every effort and achievement.

God has designed a unique plan and purpose for your life that encompasses both your academic journey and athletic pursuits. Every challenge, demand, and success you encounter as a student-athlete is an opportunity to trust His timing, rely on His provision, and grow in your faith. Staying anchored in His Word and consistent in prayer equips you to remain steady when pressures mount and to persevere with confidence when obstacles arise. As you balance the classroom and the court, remember that He is not only shaping your skills and knowledge but also refining your character and preparing you for the greater calling He has set before you. Trust that He is guiding, sustaining, and directing each step along the way.

Prayer For Champions

Heavenly Father,

We come before You, aware of our limitations and our need for Your guidance. Grant us the patience and wisdom to manage the demands of our academics and athletics, and the grace to approach each responsibility with care. Help us to rely on Your direction, seek help when we falter, and trust that even our smallest efforts can honor You. May our hearts remain focused on You in all that we do. In Jesus' name, Amen.

REFLECTION

COMFORT IN GOD'S PRESENCE

For The Athlete Missing Their Family In Season

As you dedicate yourself to your athletic career and strive for excellence in your sport, it is natural to experience a profound longing for your family, especially when living away from home, whether as a college athlete, a professional playing overseas, or traveling extensively for competitions. The absence of familiar faces, shared meals, and everyday moments with loved ones can weigh heavily on your heart, stirring feelings of loneliness, homesickness, and emotional strain. In these moments, it is essential to remember that God sees every ache, understands every longing, and offers His presence as a source of comfort and peace.

During seasons of separation, Scripture offers a powerful truth: *"The Lord is close to the brokenhearted and saves those who are crushed in spirit." (Psalm 34:18)*. When the silence of an empty room feels heavier than the noise of a packed arena, or when distance intensifies the ache for home, God draws near. He is neither distant from your struggle nor unaware of your pain. His presence surrounds you with a love that comforts, a strength that sustains, and a peace that carries you through the weight of loneliness. What family cannot provide in those moments, He graciously supplies, reminding us that even far from home, we are never far from Him.

Turn to God in prayer and rely on His unfailing love to sustain you during times when you long for your family's presence. Remember that He is with you, comforting you and providing the strength to persevere through the challenges of separation. Although physical distance may keep you apart from your family, know that your bond with them transcends the miles. Keep them close in your thoughts and prayers, trusting that God is watching over both them and you, bridging the gap with His divine presence and love.

As you continue on your athletic journey, hold firmly to the hope of reuniting with your family. Though the miles may create distance, they cannot sever the bond of love that God has placed between you and those you cherish. Until the day of togetherness arrives, treasure the memories that sustain you, nurture your connection through every call and message, and rest in the assurance that God's love weaves your hearts together across every mile. In His presence, separation does not diminish love; it strengthens it.

Prayer For Champions

Heavenly Father,

We offer You our feelings of loneliness and the longing we carry for our families. Hold our loved ones close to our hearts, and grant us Your peace and comfort during this time of separation. Help us find rest in Your presence and trust in Your promise that You will never leave us nor forsake us. Strengthen us with Your love and grace as we navigate the challenges of being apart from those we hold dear. In Jesus' name, we pray, Amen.

REFLECTION

FINDING HOPE IN GOD THROUGH STRUGGLES

When Faith And Performance Collide

In the world of sports, where every game carries significance and every performance feels like a measure of your worth, it is natural to wrestle with questions when situations don't go as planned. The sting of failure, the pressure of expectations, and the fear of disappointing others can leave you wondering where God is through it all. Yet, even in those difficult moments, His presence has not abandoned you. Your worth has never been tied to your statistics or the scoreboard; it rests securely in who you are as a child of God. In Him, you find a hope that endures beyond every struggle, setback, and season.

In Romans 5:3-5, the apostle Paul reminds us of the transformative power of suffering and perseverance: *"Not only so, but we also glory in our sufferings, because we know that suffering produces perseverance; perseverance, character; and character, hope. And hope does not put us to shame because God's love has been poured out into our hearts through the Holy Spirit who has been given to us."* These verses offer a perspective shift, inviting us to see struggles not as signs of God's absence, but as opportunities for growth and greater reliance on His grace.

Regardless of your performance on the court, God's love

for you remains steadfast and unwavering. This love is unconditional, not dependent on statistics, highlights, or the approval of fans and coaches. Instead, He looks beyond the scoreboard and the opinions of others, seeing the fullness of who you are: His son or daughter, created in His image and redeemed through Christ.

In times of disappointment and doubt, we must remember that God can bring meaning and purpose even out of the most difficult circumstances. Struggles are not wasted moments; they are refining seasons through which He shapes our character and refines our faith. Rather than viewing challenges as setbacks, we can see them as opportunities for growth; moments when perseverance is strengthened, humility is learned, and reliance on God is fortified. Through every trial, He molds us into the men and women He has called us to be, ensuring that our lives reflect His glory far more than our own achievements.

Today, let go of the pressure to perform perfectly, and instead, rest in the knowledge that your identity is rooted in Christ. Embrace the journey of growth and perseverance, knowing that God is with you every step of the way.

Prayer For Champions

Hevenly Father,

In moments of doubt and uncertainty, we turn to You for strength and guidance. Help us anchor ourselves in Your unchanging love and grace, regardless of our performance on the court. Grant us the courage to bring our struggles to You in prayer, trusting that You are always listening and ready to comfort us. Thank You for Your faithfulness and presence in every season of our lives. In Jesus' name, Amen.

REFLECTION

PRIORITIZE YOUR TIME WITH GOD

Finding Time For God With A Demanding Schedule

In the fast-paced world of basketball, where every second feels accounted for and the demands of competition never seem to slow, it can be tempting to let your relationship with God drift into the background. Practices, games, and constant responsibilities easily crowd out quiet moments with Him. However, it is precisely within this busyness that prioritizing time with God becomes essential. In His presence, you gain the strength to endure, the peace to remain steady, and the wisdom to navigate both the challenges of the court and the greater battles of life.

Jesus addressed the pull of daily worries and competing priorities with a clear directive that speaks directly to our lives today. In Matthew 6:33, He says, *"Seek the Kingdom of God above all else, and live righteously, and he will give you everything you need."* This command is not just an instruction but a framework for how we should order our time and focus. It reminds us that when God is placed first; above the noise, the pressures, and even our ambitions, everything else falls into its proper place. By choosing to give Him our attention and devotion, we invite His guidance, provision, and sustaining grace into every part of our journey.

The question then becomes: *how do we genuinely make*

space for God amid demanding schedules and constant responsibilities? It begins with intentionality; a deliberate choice to create moments of connection with Him, even when life feels overwhelming. One practical approach is to start the day by turning your attention to God before anything else. A prayer of gratitude, a passage of Scripture, or a few quiet moments in reflection with Him can center your heart and mind, grounding you in His presence before the pace of the day accelerates. These seemingly small habits, when done consistently, become powerful rhythms that shape not only your schedule but also your entire outlook.

Throughout the day, be intentional about integrating your faith into every aspect of your athletic journey. Step onto the court with a heart full of gratitude, offering prayers of thanksgiving and inviting God to be present in every dribble, pass, and shot. During pauses, whether a break in practice, a timeout, or quiet moments between games, use the stillness to reflect, realign, and draw strength from His presence. These consistent acts of devotion remind you that your faith is not separate from the game you love but is the very foundation that sustains and empowers you both on and off the court.

During the busy season, your highest priority should be nurturing your growth in Christ, even as practices, games, and other responsibilities compete for your attention. Consistently spending time in God's Word anchors you in truth and equips you to handle both the pressures of competition and the challenges of daily life. Set aside intentional time each day to read, reflect on, and meditate upon Scripture, allowing God's promises to shape your heart, renew your mind, and direct your perspective. Take what you learn and put it into practice, letting Scripture influence the way you lead, serve, and compete. You might also consider starting a devotional or Bible study with teammates and coaches, building an environment of fellowship, accountability, and encouragement. This shared pursuit not only strengthens your personal walk with Christ but also unites your team around a higher purpose, reminding everyone that the ultimate goal is not simply winning games but honoring God through character, discipline, and faithfulness.

When you intentionally prioritize time with God, you begin to see how He intersects with the ordinary demands of daily life. Regular actions, such as reading Scripture, reflection of the Word, brief journaling, and moments of quiet allow His truth to guide your decisions, steady your emotions, and renew your focus amid the pressures of training, school, and competition. In moments of setback, you will find comfort; when choices emerge, you will gain clarity; and when fatigue sets in, you will receive the strength to persevere. These are not abstract promises but practical realities that become evident as you make space for Him each day.

Your relationship with Christ is not just an item on a checklist but the foundation of who you are. When you seek Him first, your priorities realign: performance becomes service, ambition is shaped by humility, and success is measured by faithfulness rather than by a scoreboard. Expect to experience God's faithfulness through clearer direction, renewed discipline, steadier confidence, and opportunities that advance His purposes for your life.

Prayer For Champions

Heavenly Father,

Help us to order our lives so that time with You becomes our highest priority, seeking Your presence above every distraction and demand. Grant us the discipline to meet with You daily through prayer, consistently study Scripture, and fellowship with others who strengthen our faith. Teach us to build every decision, pursuit, and effort on the foundation of our relationship with You, knowing that apart from You, we can accomplish nothing of lasting value. Strengthen and sustain us through every challenge we face on the court, in the classroom, with life, and remind us that true success is not measured by achievements but by walking faithfully with You. May our hearts remain devoted to Your will, our minds attuned to Your Word, and our lives reflect Your love and truth. In Jesus' name, Amen.

REFLECTION

FINDING CONFIDENCE IN GOD

For The Athlete Struggling To Maintain Confidence

Confidence on the court is not always easy to maintain. Every game presents its own set of challenges; whether it is a tough matchup, the pressure of a close score, or the weight of expectations from coaches, teammates, and even yourself. These moments can stir doubt and insecurity, leaving you questioning your performance and abilities. A missed shot, a costly turnover, or a relentless opponent can shake even the strongest sense of assurance when that confidence is built solely on performance. However, the truth is that real confidence cannot rest on fluctuating outcomes or temporary successes. Beyond the ups and downs of competition lies a greater and more enduring foundation: your identity in Christ. When you recognize that your worth is secured in Him, you no longer play simply to prove yourself; you play with freedom, knowing that your value does not rise or fall with the scoreboard. This confidence, rooted in who you are in Christ, remains steady through both triumphs and setbacks, enabling you to compete with boldness, resilience, and joy regardless of the circumstances.

In 2 Corinthians 3:4-5, Paul declares, *"Such confidence we have through Christ before God. Not that we are competent in ourselves to claim anything for ourselves, but our competence comes from God."* Paul emphasizes that true confidence does not originate from our own abilities, achievements, or track record; it flows solely from Christ. For athletes, this means that your identity and worth are not determined by how many points you score, whether you make the starting lineup, or how flawless your performance appears. Confidence based solely on skill will always fluctuate with circumstances, but confidence anchored in Christ remains steady and secure because it rests on who He is, not on what you do.

When doubts begin to surface, it is essential to redirect our focus away from our limited abilities and toward the unchanging promises of God and the truth of our identity in Him. Left unchecked, insecurity feeds on missed opportunities, mistakes, or comparisons with others, but God calls us to view ourselves through His perspective instead of our own. His Word reminds us that we are chosen, loved, and equipped with everything we need to face the challenges before us, both on and off the court. Instead of dwelling on shortcomings or replaying failures, we are invited to fix our eyes on the assurance that our value does not depend on flawless performance but on Christ's finished work. In Him, we are strengthened for every trial, sustained through every test, and empowered to compete with confidence that flows not from our talent alone but from the God who has already secured the ultimate victory.

As you navigate the highs and lows of your athletic journey, remember that your talents, skills, and opportunities are not random or self-made; they are gifts entrusted to you by God to glorify Him. Every ability you possess, from your physical strength to your mental focus, is part of His design and calling for your life. Whether your performance results in victory or defeat, the outcome does not diminish His sovereignty over your path or His presence in every moment of competition. You never step onto the court alone, nor do you rely solely on your own strength to endure the demands of the game. God equips you with endurance, sustains you in moments of weakness, and empowers you to face obstacles that might otherwise seem overwhelming. True confidence is built not on personal achievement or external recognition but on the assurance that God is working through you. When you embrace this perspective, you realize that every practice, game, and challenge is part of a greater story; one in which your effort and faithfulness become instruments of His purpose both on and off the court.

Fear and self-doubt should never be the voices that dictate how you compete. The pressures of the game, the weight of expectations, and the sting of mistakes may tempt you to question your ability or worth, but these are not the truths that define you. It is precisely in the moments when pressure is greatest and failures seem most costly that you are called to choose perseverance, resilience, and trust in God's plan over the lies of insecurity. Confidence does not come from denying challenges or pretending weakness doesn't exist; it grows as you confront adversity with the assurance that your value is already secured in Christ. When your identity rests in Him, you are free to compete with boldness and courage—not because of flawless execution, but because you belong to the Most High God, who has already declared your worth and sealed your victory in Christ.

Prayer For Champions

Heavenly Father,

In moments when doubt and insecurity weigh heavily on our hearts, remind us of the secure identity we have in You. Guard us against the temptation to measure our worth by performance, achievements, or the opinions of others. Instead, anchor our confidence in Your unfailing love and sustaining grace. Strengthen us through the power of Your

Spirit, granting us the courage to stand firm, the resilience to endure trials, and the faith to press forward with perseverance. Equip us to face every challenge, whether on the court or in life, with boldness that flows not from ourselves, but from the assurance of who we are in Christ. May this foundation steady our minds, empower our efforts, and ensure that all we do honors You. In Jesus' name, Amen.

REFLECTION

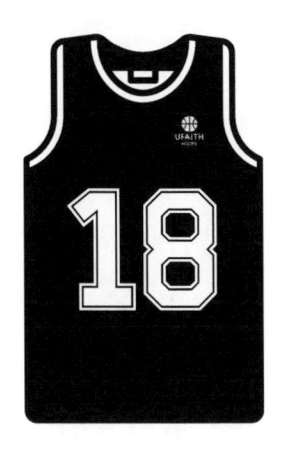

SEEKING UNITY AND PEACE WITHIN TEAM

Guide For Perseverance Through Team Conflict

Conflict is not a matter of if, but when, in the life of any team. Different personalities, competing ambitions, and high-pressure environments create moments of tension that no athlete can avoid. What matters most is not the presence of conflict, but the response to it. Left unchecked, even small disagreements can erode trust, divide teammates, and weaken the pursuit of a common goal. However, when handled with wisdom and humility, those same moments become opportunities for growth, both for the individual and for the team as a whole. God calls us to a higher standard: to be peacemakers who pursue unity through intentional love, patient listening, and selfless humility. By surrendering pride and choosing understanding, we open the door to forgiveness, restoration, and stronger bonds of trust.

Scripture provides the foundation for this calling: *"Above all, love each other deeply, because love covers over a multitude of sins." (1 Peter 4:8)*. This verse is not a suggestion for convenient moments; it is a command for every circumstance, including conflict. Love that covers does not ignore wrongdoing but chooses to respond with grace instead of resentment. It calls us to lay aside defensiveness, bitterness and prioritize reconciliation over being *"right."* On the court, this means choosing to encourage rather than criticize, listen instead of arguing, and seek understanding even when frustrations run high. This love reflects the heart of Christ and builds a foundation of trust that no disagreement can dismantle.

In the midst of team conflict, turn to God in prayer, seeking His guidance, wisdom, and peace to navigate difficult situations. Trust that He can bring reconciliation and restoration to relationships that feel strained or fractured. By relying on His direction, we are empowered to approach one another with grace, patience, and compassion, recognizing that true unity and harmony come from Him. Prayer not only strengthens our hearts but also equips us to act in ways that honor God and build a stronger, more cohesive team.

Take an honest look at your actions, words, attitudes, and consider how they may be influencing the team dynamic. Growth begins with personal accountability. A willingness to self-evaluate creates space for humility and maturity, both of which are essential for building trust. At the same time, healthy communication must remain central. Listen attentively, not simply waiting for your turn to respond. When you speak, do so with clarity and respect, aiming to strengthen, not divide. Instead of pushing for individual advantage, seek solutions that elevate the entire team. This approach not only resolves immediate tension but also lays the foundation for lasting collaboration and respect.

Always approach conflict resolution with patience and empathy, recognizing that each teammate brings a unique perspective shaped by their experiences, emotions, and expectations. Understanding these differences allows you to respond thoughtfully rather than react impulsively, creating an environment of respect and collaboration. By actively listening, seeking to understand others' viewpoints, and communicating with humility, you create opportunities to build trust and strengthen relationships. Approaching disagreements in this way not only promotes harmony within the team but also exemplifies maturity, leadership, and the character of Christ in action. Through empathy and intentional dialogue, conflicts can become opportunities for growth, unity, and stronger connection both on and off the court.

Additionally, consider seeking guidance from a mentor, coach, or counselor to provide insight and support as you navigate through conflict with your teammates. Having a trusted and impartial third party to offer perspective and advice can help you gain new insights, develop effective strategies for conflict resolution, and strengthen your relationships within the team.

In moments of conflict, prioritize the well-being of the team and its shared goals over personal disagreements. When your focus remains on the greater mission, unity and purpose can overcome the challenges that seek to divide. Rely on God's wisdom to guide your responses, trusting that He will provide the clarity and strength needed for reconciliation and understanding. As you navigate conflict, remember that God's presence is constant, and His desire is to see your team strengthened through peace, humility, and a commitment to collaboration.

Prayer For Champions

Heavenly Father,

We come before You as one team, seeking Your wisdom and strength in moments of conflict and challenge. Teach us to set aside pride and selfish ambition and instead pursue understanding, patience, and love toward one another. Help us to see our teammates as You see them; valuable, gifted, and worthy of respect. When disagreements arise, remind us to listen with humility, speak with grace, and seek solutions that strengthen our unity. Guard our hearts against division, and fill us with a spirit of forgiveness that reflects the love Christ has shown us. May our commitment to peace and unity be a testimony of Your presence in our lives, both on and off the court. In Jesus' name, Amen.

REFLECTION

OVERCOMING BAD HABITS OFF THE COURT

Conquering Off-Court Challenges With Grace

Struggling with bad habits off the court is more than a personal inconvenience; it is a challenge that affects your character, focus, and even your performance as an athlete. These habits, whether subtle or destructive, can quietly weaken discipline and hinder growth. That is why they cannot be ignored or excused. Overcoming them requires more than willpower alone; it requires inviting God into the process. His grace is not only sufficient for salvation but also powerful enough to break cycles, restore discipline, and strengthen every area of your life.

This is why Romans 12:2 speaks with such clarity: *"Do not conform to the pattern of this world, but be transformed by the renewing of your mind. Then you will be able to test and approve what God's will is—his good, pleasing, and perfect will."* As a Believer, you are not called to follow the world's patterns or indulge in its distractions; you are called to live set apart. Transformation begins when you allow God to reshape your mind and habits. By surrendering old patterns, you make room for His will to guide you into freedom, discipline, and lasting strength.

Overcoming destructive habits is not meant to be faced in isolation. Seeking accountability from a trusted mentor, coach, or fellow Believer can provide the encouragement and perspective you need when the struggle feels overwhelming. God often works through others to strengthen us, offering wisdom, correction, and support at critical moments. Alongside accountability, turn daily to God in prayer. Ask Him for the strength to resist temptation, the discernment to make wise choices, and the courage to walk in obedience. When you lean on both the fellowship of others and the faithfulness of God, you are equipped to replace harmful patterns with habits that bring honor to Him and align with His will.

As you commit to surrendering your struggles to God and seeking His transformation in your life, trust that He is faithful to walk alongside you every step of the way. Through His grace and power, you can break free from negative habits and live a life that reflects His love and glory. Remember that breaking free from these habits is a process that requires patience, perseverance, and a reliance on His strength. As you navigate this journey, it's important to be gentle with yourself and understand that setbacks may occur. Trust in God's faithfulness to guide you back on the right path and empower you to make positive changes in your life.

James 4:7-8 provides a clear directive for those struggling with destructive habits: *"Submit yourselves, then, to God. Resist the devil, and he will flee from you. Come near to God and he will come near to you..."* Breaking free from unhealthy patterns requires more than willpower; it demands submission to God's authority and reliance on His presence. As you draw close to Him in prayer, immerse yourself in Scripture, and engage in authentic worship, you invite His power to work within you. In that closeness, He provides the peace to calm your restlessness and the strength to stand firm against temptation, enabling you to make choices that reflect His will and lead to lasting transformation.

Remember that God's love and grace surpass every struggle you face. His promise to renew your mind and empower your choices ensures that you can live a life reflecting His goodness, mercy, and truth. Allow His Spirit to guide your thoughts, actions, and decisions, leading you away from destructive habits and toward a path of righteousness and integrity.

Approach the journey of transformation with steadfast hope and unwavering faith, fully confident that God walks with you every step of the way. His enduring love never falters, and His grace is more than sufficient to sustain you through challenges, setbacks, and moments of uncertainty. By surrendering completely to His will, you invite Him to work within your mind, shaping your thoughts; within your character, refining your choices; and within your spirit, strengthening your resolve and anchoring your identity in Him. Transformation is not instantaneous, but as you remain faithful and receptive, God orchestrates growth that is everlasting, equipping you to handle trials, lead with integrity, and embrace your calling. Trusting in His timing and methods, you can navigate every stage of change with courage, resilience, and the assurance that His purposes are perfect and His faithfulness endures.

Prayer For Champions

Heavenly Father,

We come before You with humble hearts, recognizing the struggles, distractions, and patterns that hinder our growth both on and off the court. Grant us the strength, wisdom, and courage to confront these habits honestly and to pursue Your transformative work in every aspect of our lives. Help us resist temptation, make decisions that honor You, and consistently reflect Your goodness through our words, actions, and attitudes. May Your grace sustain us in moments of weakness, empower us to persevere when challenges arise, and guide our steps as we intentionally break free from anything that obstructs Your purposes. Enable us to walk fully in alignment with Your will, trusting that each choice made in obedience strengthens our character, sharpens our focus, and glorifies You. In Jesus' name, Amen.

REFLECTION

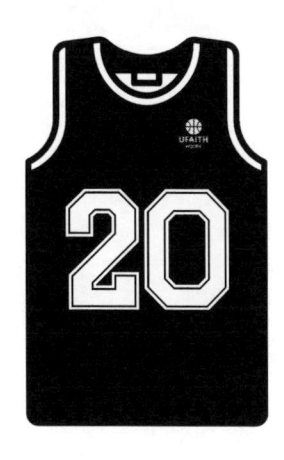

FINDING STRENGTH IN DEFEAT

Rise Again

Defeat is an inescapable reality for every competitor. It arrives in the sting of a missed shot, the heartbreak of a loss, or the silence that follows a season-ending injury. In those moments, the scoreboard feels louder than your own heartbeat, and the weight of disappointment presses heavily on your spirit. Yet, defeat is not the end; it is a proving ground. It dismantles illusions, challenges your pride, and forces you to confront who you are beyond performance. More than any victory, it is in defeat that faith is tested, character is revealed, and the foundation of true resilience is built.

In the aftermath of defeat, a range of emotions often arises: disappointment, frustration, discouragement, and even anger. These reactions are not signs of weakness; they reveal the depth of your passion, the seriousness of your commitment, and the significance of the effort you have invested. While it is natural to experience these emotions, it is essential not to let them take root unchecked, as they can fuel negativity and hinder both personal and athletic growth. Defeat is not meant to define you or imprison your spirit; it is intended to teach, refine, and redirect you. By reflecting on what went wrong, learning from mistakes, and leaning on God for guidance, you can transform disappointment into discernment, frustration into focus, and setbacks into opportunities for resilience, perseverance, and renewed purpose. In this way, every loss becomes a stepping stone, preparing you to compete with greater wisdom, humility, and determination.

Instead of allowing defeat to define your worth or dictate your mindset, turn to God as your unwavering source of strength and stability. He is your rock and refuge when circumstances feel uncertain, when pressure increases, or when failure threatens to overwhelm you. As Psalm 34:18 reminds us, *"The Lord is close to the brokenhearted and saves those who are crushed in spirit."* Even in the depths of disappointment, His presence remains steadfast, offering comfort, perspective, and renewed courage. Defeat, therefore, becomes more than a moment of discouragement; it becomes a classroom where God teaches resilience, patience, and reliance on Him. Take time to reflect on what the experience reveals: perhaps it is a call to embrace humility, identify and strengthen areas of weakness, refine your preparation, or depend more fully on His guidance. Every setback carries within it the potential for a comeback when you allow God to shape your response, redirect your focus, and establish perseverance, wisdom, and character that will serve you both on and off the court.

Draw strength and encouragement from the examples of perseverance found throughout Scripture. Consider Job, who endured unimaginable loss and suffering, yet remained steadfast in his faith and devotion to God. His story reminds us that even in the darkest valleys, when circumstances feel overwhelming or hopeless, faith has the power to endure and sustain us. James 1:2-3 instructs us to adopt this perspective: *"Consider it pure joy, my brothers and sisters, whenever you face trials of many kinds, because you know that the testing of your faith produces perseverance."* These verses do not dismiss or minimize the pain, struggle, or disappointment inherent in trials; rather, they call us to view adversity as an opportunity for growth. Each challenge becomes a means to refine our character, deepen our reliance on God, and anchor our trust in His wisdom and sovereignty. By studying the faithful examples in Scripture and embracing God's guidance, we learn that perseverance is not merely enduring hardship but actively allowing trials to shape us into resilient, disciplined, and Christ-centered individuals, prepared to face future challenges with courage and unwavering hope.

Finally, never forget that your identity is not defined by your performance, wins, or statistics on the court. You are a beloved child of God, fearfully and wonderfully made in His image, and your ultimate purpose is to glorify Him in every action, decision, and pursuit. When defeat comes, when mistakes feel costly, or when outcomes fall short of your expectations, stand firm in the assurance that God remains sovereign over every aspect of your life. His plans for you extend far beyond any setback, disappointment, or temporary failure, and He is actively at work shaping your character, perseverance, and faithfulness through every circumstance. Grounded in this truth, you can approach each challenge with confidence, resilience, and the knowledge that your worth and purpose are secure in Him, independent of the scoreboard or public recognition.

Prayer For Champions

Heavenly Father,

In moments of defeat, we come before You, honestly acknowledging our pain, disappointment, and the weight of our struggles. Strengthen us when we feel broken, restore our confidence when it falters, and guide our steps when uncertainty threatens to overwhelm us. Help us to view every setback not as a measure of failure but as an opportunity to grow in character, learn valuable lessons, and lean more fully on Your wisdom and provision. Teach us to remain humble in victory, resilient in loss, and steadfast in faith regardless of circumstances. May Your presence bring enduring peace to our hearts, clarity to our minds, and courage to persevere through challenges. Use every trial to refine our character, increase our trust in You, and draw us ever closer to Your purposes. In Jesus' name, Amen.

REFLECTION

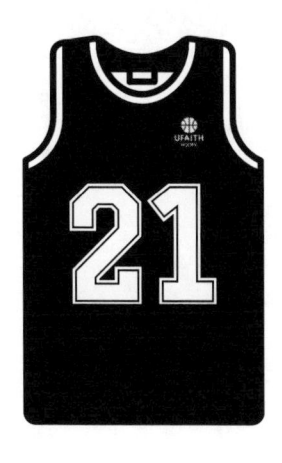

SOARING ON WINGS OF FAITH

For The Athlete Struggling With Motivation

There are times when maintaining motivation feels like an uphill battle. The relentless demands of training, the pressure to perform at peak levels, and the weight of expectations can leave even the most disciplined athlete feeling drained and discouraged. However, for those who follow Christ, strength and motivation come from a source far greater than personal willpower or determination. By anchoring ourselves in His promises and relying on His guidance, we can develop motivation that is resilient, purposeful, and enduring. In Christ, even seasons of weariness can become moments of renewal, shaping us to endure with joy and purpose.

Renewed motivation begins with surrendering our burdens to the Lord. Many people try to rely on personal drive or determination to push through difficult seasons, but lasting strength cannot be built on self-reliance. True endurance is created when we place our full trust in God, allowing His power to sustain us where our own energy falls short. When motivation fades, the proper response is to turn to Him in prayer, seeking His guidance, strength, and peace to persevere with purpose.

Reflecting on God's faithfulness throughout our lives provides powerful motivation to persevere. When we take time to remember how He has guided us through past obstacles, supplied strength in moments of weakness, and opened doors when circumstances seemed closed, we are reminded that His provision has never failed. The same God who carried us before will continue to uphold us in our present challenges and sustain us in those yet to come. By anchoring ourselves in His promises and choosing to rest in His presence, we draw from a source of strength that does not waver with changing circumstances or fluctuating emotions.

This perspective shifts our motivation away from the temporary pressures of performance and toward the eternal assurance of His unchanging love and purpose. For athletes, this means approaching each practice, game, and season not with anxiety over outcomes but with confidence that God's hand is at work, shaping both our character and our journey. In this way, faith becomes the foundation that fuels perseverance, resilience, and a renewed commitment to press forward in every area of life and competition.

Motivation also increases when we understand the greater purpose behind our pursuits. The ultimate aim is not personal recognition, applause, or temporary achievements, but faithfully using every gift and ability to glorify God. When athletic efforts are guided by this perspective, even the most demanding challenges take on new meaning. Difficult practices become opportunities to demonstrate discipline and commitment, competitions become platforms to reflect integrity and perseverance, and setbacks become moments to reveal resilience and trust in God's plan. In this way, every aspect of the athletic journey, whether victory or defeat, serves as an expression of worship, pointing others to the God who provides both strength and purpose.

Another key source of motivation is the strength found in community. Walking alongside fellow Believers creates an environment of encouragement, accountability, and support that sustains us through difficult seasons. Within this fellowship, we pray for one another, speak truth in love, and continually remind each other of God's faithfulness. Together, we are stronger and better equipped to stay focused on the purpose God has set before us.

Furthermore, establishing consistent habits that integrate faith into training strengthens both motivation and focus by keeping God at the center of the athletic journey. This can be as intentional as beginning each practice with prayer, reflecting on Scripture during workouts, or using moments of training to meditate on God's promises. Even something as simple as listening to worship music while preparing for competition can shift the heart and mind toward Him. These actions remind athletes that time on the court is not separate from their walk with God but is an extension of it. Every drill, repetition, and game becomes an opportunity to honor Him, transforming training from a physical routine into an act of worship that fuels perseverance and aligns performance with His greater purpose.

Let us remain anchored in the power that comes from God, trusting Him to renew our strength and sustain us through every challenge. When He becomes our source of strength, no obstacle is too great, and no setback is final. With our eyes fixed on Him, we can rise with endurance, compete with purpose, and fulfill the calling He has placed on our lives.

Prayer For Champions

Heavenly Father,

Thank you for being our source of strength and motivation. In moments of weariness and doubt, help us turn to you, surrendering our burdens and finding renewed hope in your promises. Remind us of your faithfulness in the past, and guide us as we strive to honor you in our athletic pursuits. May our actions both on and off of the court bring glory to your name. In Jesus' name, Amen.

REFLECTION

FINDING STRENGTH IN RECOVERY

A Devotional For The Athlete Returning From Injury

Resilience in the face of injury is a significant demonstration of strength. Being sidelined affects more than just physical performance; it challenges your focus, patience, and faith. Absence from competition often brings frustration, discouragement, and uncertainty about when or how you will return to the game you love. Even in these difficult seasons, however, God provides an opportunity to rely fully on Him. Recovery is not solely about restoring physical ability but also about allowing God to strengthen your spirit, sharpen your perspective, and anchor your trust in His perfect plan.

During recovery, it is natural to feel impatience, doubt, or even discouragement; however, these moments can serve as powerful opportunities for growth. Each setback challenges you to examine your mindset, refine your discipline, and increase your reliance on God's guidance. Progress may be gradual, and the process uncomfortable, yet every step, whether small or significant, strengthens your resilience and shapes your character. By embracing this season with faith and intentionality, you allow God not only to restore your body but also to develop perseverance, perspective, and unwavering trust in His timing.

As you work toward returning to your sport, it is

important to remain focused on the present moment and to approach each day with discipline, patience, and trust. Recovery is neither quick nor effortless; it often requires enduring discomfort, facing setbacks, and embracing routines that challenge both your body and tenacity. Yet, progress is made through steady commitment; by adhering to your rehabilitation plan, listening to the guidance of medical professionals, and paying close attention to the signals your body sends. Each exercise, stretch, and adjustment, though it may seem small in isolation, plays a vital role in restoring strength, stability, and readiness for competition.

Viewing recovery as part of your overall athletic journey, rather than an interruption, allows you to appreciate its value in shaping resilience and perseverance. When you entrust this process to God, you can move through it with peace and confidence, knowing that He is present at every step. The progress you make under His care is preparing you to return to your sport stronger, more focused, and fully ready to perform at your best.

Be intentional in practicing patience and extending grace to yourself at every stage. Setbacks, fatigue, and moments of frustration are natural, but they do not have to derail your progress. Instead, channel these emotions into focused effort, disciplined action, and renewed determination to follow your rehabilitation plan consistently. Maintain a clear vision of your full return to the court and let that vision guide your daily efforts. By approaching recovery with both diligence and self-compassion, you transform challenges into opportunities to build resilience, strengthen mental toughness, and prepare yourself to reenter competition fully equipped to meet the demands of your sport.

As you navigate the recovery process, recognize that every challenge, delay, and moment of frustration presents an opportunity to grow; not only physically, but also mentally and emotionally. Lean fully on God's strength, trusting that He is present and guiding every step, even when progress seems slow or uncertain. Allow this season to shape your mindset, grow your dependence on Him, and strengthen your character, perseverance, and resilience in ways that extend far beyond the court. Recovery is not just a return to physical performance; it is a transformative period during which God prepares you to approach your sport, your relationships, and your life with renewed purpose, perspective, and faith. Embrace each moment with intentionality, knowing that every effort, setback, and small victory is part of God's work to mold you into the athlete and person He created you to be.

Prayer For Champions

Heavenly Father,

Guide us through every stage of this recovery process, providing the strength, focus, and perseverance necessary to regain our full potential. Let this period of physical limitation become a deliberate opportunity to refine our discipline, resilience, and trust in Your plan. Equip us to maintain a consistent mindset of determination and purpose, even when progress is slow or setbacks occur. Remind us of the dedication and passion that brought us to our sport, and help us channel that energy into intentional growth and preparation for the challenges ahead.

Protect our hearts from discouragement and help us recognize Your presence in every effort, every challenge, and every small victory along the way. Restore our bodies with Your healing power while shaping our character, strengthening our resilience, and developing our commitment to excellence in all that we do. Grant us clarity to make wise decisions, courage to persevere through obstacles, and steadfastness to remain faithful to the process, trusting that You are actively at work in every stage of this journey. May we rely fully on Your guidance, remain disciplined in our efforts, and honor You through both our progress and our setbacks. In Jesus' name, Amen.

REFLECTION

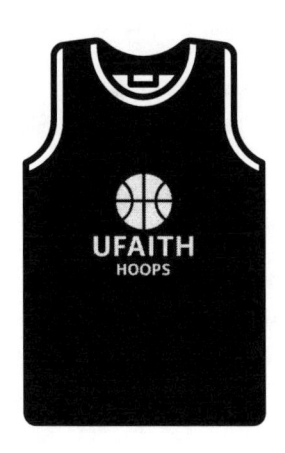

Thank you for joining us in *Courtside Devotion*, where we have explored how faith can intersect with our athletic endeavors. As we close this devotional, we hope that you have been encouraged to strengthen your relationship with God, both on and off the court. Remember, through Him, all things are possible. Keep seeking Him in all that you do, and may your faith continue to guide and inspire you in your athletic journey.

As you reflect on the words of this devotional, remember that you are never alone in your athletic journey. God is with you every step of the way, providing strength, wisdom, and guidance in both victory and struggle. Rely on Him in moments of triumph and during seasons of challenge, allowing His unfailing love to be the foundation of your confidence, courage, and perseverance.

In the demanding world of sports, it is tempting to lose sight of what truly matters. As you strive for excellence on the court, remember that your identity and worth are not determined by your performance or achievements. You are a beloved child of God, created in His image and valued beyond measure. Let this truth anchor you in times of doubt and uncertainty.

As you continue to pursue your athletic goals, remember the importance of rest and renewal both on and off the court. Just as your body requires recovery to perform at its best, your walk with God also needs intentional time through prayer, reflection on His Word, and moments spent in His presence. When you pause to seek Him, He restores your strength, refreshes your heart, and prepares you to face the journey ahead with faith, endurance, and confidence in His guidance.

As you navigate the ups and downs of your athletic journey, surround yourself with a community of fellow Believers who can support and encourage you along the way. Whether it's teammates, coaches, or friends from your community, having a support system can make all the difference in staying grounded and resilient in the face of challenges.

Remember that success in sports is not measured solely by wins and losses, but by the character and integrity with which you play the game. Let your actions on the court reflect the values of humility, perseverance, and sportsmanship that honor God and inspire those around you.

When you step off the court and enter the world beyond the game, carry the lessons found in this devotional with you. Faith is meant to shape every aspect of life; not only athletics but also relationships, academics, career, and every opportunity placed before you. Walk with boldness and confidence, assured that God has already equipped you with the strength, wisdom, and perseverance needed to fulfill His purpose for your life.

God bless you. May you play with passion and purpose, always knowing you are never alone. In Jesus' name, Amen.